SIMPLE THOUGHTS

Xavier Grice

iUniverse LLC
Bloomington

Simple Thoughts

iUniverse books may be ordered through booksellers or by contacting:

iUniverse LLC
1663 Liberty Drive
Bloomington, IN 47403
www.iuniverse.com
1-800-Authors (1-800-288-4677)

ISBN: 978-1-4759-9835-1 (sc)
ISBN: 978-1-4759-9836-8 (ebk)

Library of Congress Control Number: 2013912466

Printed in the United States of America

iUniverse rev. date: 07/11/2013

SIMPLE THOUGHTS

Contents

Preface..vii

Dedication ix

Chapter 1 1
    Money What Is It? 3
    Paper Chasers 5
    Little Girls 6
    Sex Games 7

Chapter 2 9
    Respect..11
    Do Unto Others 12
    Are You Better Than Anyone Else..................................13
    Evil Intentions..14

Chapter 3 15
    Be Confident 17
    Happiness 18
    Love Train 19
    Lonely People 20
    Pain 21
    Uncertainty 22
    Selfishness 23
    Move On 24

Chapter 4 25
    Different Thinking 27
    Men's Thinking 28
    Cuss Words 29
    If 30
    Parenthood 31
    Not As Evolved 32

Closed Doors 33
Complicated...34
Skin Deep 35

Chapter 5 37
Youth Sports 39
College Football Scandals 40
Paying Attention To Details 41
Know It All's 42
Wants Vs Needs 43
Swag 44
Wasted Potential..45
New Generation 47

Chapter 6 49
Dream 51
Co-Pilot 52
A Person's Heart 53
Good Will 54
Tested 55
Emergency Brakes 56
Life Lessons 57
Birth Control 58
Hostage 59

Chapter 7 61
Suggestions for the Economic Recovery 63
Budget Cuts 64
Political Surprises 65
Elections 66
Educated Arrogance 67
Millionaire Job Hunting 68
Burger King or Bust 69
Corporate Takeover 70
No Retirement 71
Technology...72
Why...73

Preface

I am not an English Major or a journalist. What I am is an average working stiff sharing his observations and opinions of things happening in this world of ours. So hopefully the run on sentences and not so correct structure still gets the point across to readers. I hope you enjoy and some of it makes you think in a different way after reading it.

Dedication

This book or essays is dedicated to my family. They are the reason I get up in the morning. Some of the thoughts were inspired just by being around you guys. Love you guys.

CHAPTER 1

Money What Is It?

Mankind's slow development as a species has to do with money, or the bartering and exchange of goods and services. We as humans would be much more advanced as a race of beings if we all just worked together. But for right now we haven't evolved enough, mentally or emotionally. First if we emotionally evolve, then the rest should come into place. But as long as greed and jealousy are a part of us, we will only make small strides when we could be making great leaps. Money what is it? Just paper, it doesn't move on it's on. It doesn't do anything in particular. Why do we value it so much? Why do we have to have more than the next person? Why as people do we want it? I will tell you why, to buy things. To accumulate things to show or make us feel we are better than the next person. Just think about this for a second. One car costs $15,000 and the other costs $250,000. Assuming the quality of one is better than the other. What I am about to explain is why we won't see other planets or do more amazing things in our lifetime. Both cars have 4 tires, 1 engine, doors and windows. Guess what both cars are crap. Here is the reason why. Both cars were built to break down to keep you spending money on them and putting money in other people's hands. Why can't we build tires we don't have to replace every few thousand miles? There are multiple parts on a car that are meant to break to keep you coming back to get them repaired or replaced. What a waste of resources. We have the knowledge to build shelter and transportation that wouldn't require constant maintenance. But this little thing called greed won't let that take place. Because of greed the pursuit of money will be the top priority of many of us. All of us have unique skills we could use. If everyone used their gifts and talents with people of similar interests and work together the possibilities are limitless. If we could only evolve past the greed and jealousy! Remember the saying whatever we can imagine the mind can achieve. Just a simple thought.

Paper Chasers

Some women think they are smarter than men because they are using a man to get material things. These women fail to realize that the man knows that she is using him. This man and men like him don't really care about the material things. These things are just tools they are using to get these women to give away their bodies and self-respect. So ladies who are paper chasers of this kind who think they are outsmarting these men, think again. Because they just want sex and you have outsmarted yourself by giving it to them. Just a simple thought.

Little Girls

Girls take the advice of a 40 something man. Stop making yourselves a number or a notch on some boy's belt. I was a young man at one point in my life. I have a teenage daughter who is smart and beautiful. When boys see you wearing those revealing clothes and make-up to look older you know what they are thinking? I like her and I want to see if she has a good personality. NOT!!!!!! They are thinking how can I get some of her and see her naked. They are not thinking she looks nice and I want to ask her out on a date. No he wants to ask you out of your clothes the little you have on. If you give it to him he is not going to ask you to be his girlfriend. You just became bragging rights for him to his buddies. Most boys or men today are not gentlemen. They will tell their buddies. Most guys as the saying goes "can't hold water". When you see each other in the mall and pass one another. He will smile at you and you will smile back, but as soon as you are out of ear shot he will tell his buddies ya'll I hit that. Now they will look at you differently and try to get with you but not as a boyfriend. So now this is the beginning of your reputation turning to mud. Girls respect yourselves and dress and act your age. Make the guys know the young lady and not the girl with the revealing clothes. Once guys really get to know you their thinking becomes different. They become protectors and friends. A friend and someone who likes you for you and not your body is really who you should want to be with. Just a simple thought.

Sex Games

Sex is a great part of a relationship. It really makes you feel connected to a person if even for just a few moments. But in a relationship playing games with sex can be tricky to unhealthy. Don't use sex as a reward or punishment with your partner or special someone. Don't use sex as a tool to make them do what you want them to do. If a man or female is told that they are cut off until they do what you want you might not like the result. It was once said that you are being cut off because the person was being true to themselves. So not being intimate with your special person because you are being true to yourself is just bull. It was just a way to try and get what they wanted. Now unless you and your special person are Adam and Eve, meaning you are the only humans on earth. You might be true to yourself alone if not then you too will have sex or relations but not with that special person. So stop playing games with sex and enjoy your friend or spouse. Just a simple thought.

CHAPTER 2

Respect

Respect is something that is earned. Just because you have a certain rank or position doesn't mean you are respected. Respect comes with knowing how to talk to people. You can ask a person to do the most unpleasant job and they will do it. If only you ask them the right way. Now on the other hand you will have to do the job yourself if you can't ask people in a respectful manner. Lying and doing underhanded things to people also undermines respect. Once you lose the respect of your co-workers your job becomes much harder. Respect is the key. Once it's gone the lofty are headed for a fall. Just a simple thought.

Do Unto Others

When people try to do wrong to others for no apparent reason, sometimes they end up on the short end of the stick. When people misrepresent themselves to others or say one thing and do another, that too can come back on them. Be nice to people even if they aren't nice to you. It had taken me awhile to grasp this concept. People with bad intentions seem to come out on top. This is true for awhile, but it is like making a deal at the crossroads. Eventually something or someone comes to collect. When that day comes it usually is a lot worst on them than all the bad stuff that person has inflicted on others. So treat people nice and honest and the rewards will come your way. Maybe not that instant, but when you least expect it but when you need it the most. Just a simple thought.

Are You Better Than Anyone Else

Why do some of us think we are better than others? We all take a path in life. Your choices may be different than mine. But does that make you better than me. We are all the same. Some people's path may bring them frame and a lot of material wealth. Others will hardly have a penny to their name. Is the first person better than the second? No I think not and here is why! If you shoot or stab both people they would bleed red. When they die, will the first person be able to take their wealth with them? Will the second person be able to take their most prized possession with them? The answer is no. When you die you don't even take your body with you. All this nonsense we as human beings put ourselves through is pointless. For all of you out there just keep this in mind the next time you see a celebrity on television or a homeless person on the street. Just a simple thought.

Evil Intentions

Why do people have evil intentions for no apparent reasons? Everybody is trying to survive and most are living paycheck to paycheck. So the question remains what is the purpose of doing harm to someone else other than evil. Those who do bad things to others are what we sometimes called fair weather people. When all the breaks and their requests are met they are happy go lucky. If one thing goes wrong for them then they want to do harm to someone else. I am not a religious man, but everyone knows you reap what you sew. Here is a piece of advice to all the fair weather people, aka nice people impersonators. Quit being jealous, selfish and evil because when the sun is shining on you some other evil person will be waiting to do you harm. Just a simple thought.

CHAPTER 3

Be Confident

No one likes a self-pitying person. People are not attracted to the "woe is me" person. People will try to help until it gets to the point where it is found out to be just your nature all the time. Look in the mirror and do an assessment of yourself. If you see and feel there is something you don't like then change it. Don't do it for other people but for yourself. Becoming more confident you will notice a lot more opportunities begin to appear. There will be more people wanting to be around you. Your whole quality of life will change. Just a simple thought.

Happiness

No one can make you happy but you. You have to do or find the things in life that give you enjoyment. What you can do is find people who enjoy the things you do and just hang out together. This gives you someone to share your happiness. But always look within yourself for happiness and really find what you enjoy doing. Whether it be a career or recreational. Because when you look to other people to make you happy you never find it. Just a simple thought.

Love Train

Love is a strange thing. It makes you see the good in someone. It sometimes makes you see the bad. Love can make you feel light as a feather. Love also comes with other emotions like hobos on a train. So as the conductor of your love train you have to know which hobos to keep and which to kick off. Just a simple thought.

Lonely People

When people are lonely they do things out of character. They make everyday a search for companionship of some kind. Even if it is just a few words with the store clerk or the mailman. Very few people want to be alone. Most find companionship in the wrong people. The prisons and morgues are full of these unfortunate souls. Even the high divorce rate is a fact of people choosing unwisely of a companion. So if you are alone or feel alone don't rush to the first person you meet. The right person or persons are there but things take time. Think of your time alone as your special time to plan your future. Pretty soon you won't feel lonely because the good and positive people you need will suddenly be revealed. Just a simple thought.

Pain

Sometimes you have to cut the things out of your life that causes you pain. If not it will spread through your heart and eventually you will give up and die. Now doctors will say you died of natural causes. But the truth will be you died of a broken heart. Just a simple thought

Uncertainty

There is a famous quote "Life is like a box of chocolates you never know what you are going to get". This is true of people as well. When you meet a person you never know what you will get. They may become a friend for life. He or she may be a future wife or husband. They may even become an enemy. People hide emotions and intentions very well. They may have a crush on you or they may want to do you harm. Just be weary of opening the box. You really never know what you are going to get. Just a simple thought.

Selfishness

Selfishness is an ugly trait. Being selfish is also a very unattractive trait. The most physically beautiful person can become very ugly to people if their selfishness is on display all the time. There is a time and place to think of yourself first. If you put someone else first on certain things, you will see the rewards. It could be as simple as holding a door for someone. It may be giving someone change at the register. Even through you don't know that person it could make a big difference in the person's life. By helping someone else and putting them first in that moment will come back to you when you least expect it and need it the most. Other people watching you do something unselfishly may be inspired to do something themselves. You never know, you may bump into someone who witnessed your act of unselfishness. At that time they may be inclined to do something unselfish for them that will help you. Just a simple thought.

Move On

Things that happened yesterday, six months or six years ago can't be changed. You do not have to forget but you should forgive and move on. Live in the present and enjoy the moment. People can't take back or change what they did in the past. But if they try to make amends in the present, you should do the same. Life is not a guaranteed adventure. Embrace the present, turn loose the past and enjoy the moment. You may not have tomorrow to do what you have the chance to do today. Just a simple thought.

CHAPTER 4

Different Thinking

You never know how different people will react to the same information. Just because they don't do what you did doesn't make them wrong. Maybe they see handling the problem in a different way. Most problems have different solutions. All can be just as effective. Just a simple thought.

Men's Thinking

Men and women think in a totally different train of thought. Men sometimes are not the best communicators so we express in deed what we can't in words. When a man does all the things he thinks she needs, he thinks things are fine. All men are not the touchy feely guys or talkers. Taking care of bills, doing yard work and house work or buying little gifts are ways of saying what he can't say in words. Women watch your man. If he does all of the above and more he is saying I love you. He is saying you are important to him. Learn to decipher the code ladies, because feelings are not always expressed in words. Just a simple thought.

Cuss Words

Here is a question? Who decided shit, damn, asshole, were to be classified as cuss words. Have you ever asked yourself who decided this? Was there a vote or were they picked at random. They are just letters put together in a pattern just like any other words. So why are they different? Why do some people tell you that you are uneducated if you use these words. I like things simple, so just because you can spit out big words doesn't mean that you have more walking around sense than everyone else. There are different kinds of smarts. Some people are book smart. Other people are computer smart unlike me, while some people are mechanically gifted. So is using cuss words making any of these people less smart. No, so in the end a word is just a word. This is a question for the reader to answer for themselves. Just a simple thought

If

If is made up of only two letters. This word is larger than life to some people. The reason being is that everything wrong or bad in their life is because of the word if. If only this or if only that. If should be used in this sentence and it would solve most of these people's problems. If only I was motivated enough to get off my butt and do something instead of making excuses. Now when they use this sentence all of the power of this two letter word has over them would disappear. Just a simple thought.

Parenthood

Being a parent means many things. Wearing old or worn out clothing so that your children get new school clothes. Eating less to make sure they always have more than enough to eat. Working 2 sometimes 3 jobs to pay for bills and school supplies and other miscellaneous things children need. Some people forget we brought these children here. If you are not willing to make the sacrifices to take care of them, then you should not have children. If you do decide to have children do the right thing. Don't bring them in this world then change your mind and leave them to fend for themselves or have others take care of your responsibilities. I have seen the damage done to a child when left up to the system. Noting beats the love and care of a mother and father. Just a simple thought.

Not As Evolved

We humans believe we are the most evolved creatures on the planet. But if we are, why do we still act according to the same basic instincts as lesser evolved creatures. The most common one is sex drive and the desire to reproduce. In some animals there is one mate for life. In others it is the dominant male who breeds with the females. My favorites are the male animals with the brightest colors to attract the females. But in some species mating can be tricky because the females devour the male after their special time together. Some of you ladies are in this category. If you are this type of lady, don't devour those poor male suitors: just let them go. I think the one most people can relate to is the brightest or the most flashy male attracts the females. Let's think about this for a second. Why do most men crave money, fame and power? So they can buy flashy cars, big houses and expensive clothes and jewelry. Not because they dreamed of whatever job or position that got them those things, but because if gives them a larger variety of mates to choose from. Let's keep it real: would some of these fat, ugly CEO's or goofy, unattractive athletes get the same chances with the women they get if they worked selling cars or insurance? So even with all our increased brain power, we are still creatures of our basic sexual instincts. Just a simple thought.

Closed Doors

In life doors are sometimes closed just because someone thinks it is funny or just likes to make things difficult for others. Just smile and be patience because other doors will open and create better opportunities than the last. Just remember people who love to close doors for the sole purpose of flexing your muscle. One day you will be walking through a door and to your surprise guess who. One of the people you flexed your muscle on. Now that the shoe is on the other foot how would you hope they react. Just a simple thought.

Complicated

Some people think life is not complicated. For some it is not. While for others things are very complicated. Simple decisions become hard or complicated when feelings and emotions are involved. With some simple reasoning without the emotions things become clearer. Sometimes it takes time to let the emotions die down before things appear clear. So sit back, no matter how much it hurts you and give it time. Eventually all pain fades and the only thing left is reasoning. If you can hold on and not make impulse decisions with emotions of pain, love, anger or whatever emotion is driving you. Then the decision will become clear and it will be done for the right reason. Just a simple thought.

Skin Deep

Beauty is a subjective thing. What I consider beautiful may not be considered beautiful by another. But society does have a universal code of it's so called beauty. Objects are very subjective and everyone sees something different. People are a whole different ball of wax. Someone could be viewed extremely beautiful by society's standard. But their personality can destroy the look of all their outer physical beauty. A very average looking woman with a confident, friendly and loving personality can have more suitors than a supermodel. Her personality makes her inner beauty outshine the supermodel's physical beauty. So don't judge people at a first glance. That so called beautiful person could be the devil in disguise. The average looking person could be the beautiful soul mate of our dreams. Just a simple thought.

CHAPTER 5

Youth Sports

Why do coaches not care about teaching the game instead of just winning the game. If coaches taught the kids the right ways to play the game and played all of the kids, win, lose or draw the kids would get the most out of participating. Instead some kids are getting discouraged with sports because they are not all getting equal opportunity in practice or the games. Not every kid is going to be a star, but should be able to look back at their childhood and say they had a good experience playing sports. Each kid should get practice and game time for this one simple reason. How do you as a coach and role models to some know if the technique of the game you are teaching is working if all the kids don't get to participate in the games. You have the chance to be a positive or negative figure in a child's life. I would want every kid to come away from being one of my players saying they had an enjoying time and learned something from playing for me. But due to the selfishness of some coaches many kids are just losing the love for team sports because of this negative experience. Just a simple thought.

College Football Scandals

This might be taken place somewhere, but I haven't heard of where. Here is a thought, why not have a minor league football teams just like in the other big sports. I know we have the Canadian Football League and the Arena League. Those two leagues are fine, but they aren't the NFL. I understand kids coming out of high school are not physically able or ready for the NFL. But if each NFL team had it's own minor league team things would be just a little different. Here is what I propose. They play their games on Tuesday and Wednesdays. They play twelve games and have the same playoffs system as their big brother league. They would have a championship game like the Super bowl. Playing on these days will not interfere with high school on Fridays or college on Saturdays. Just think about it this way, a lot of kids go to college not for the education but for the chance to play in the NFL and it's payday. If these kids could go to the minor league for a few years, build their bodies and improve their skills while getting paid. Now that leaves the kids who want that college education to go play for their favorite college team. Don't you think that would decrease some of these college scandals? All who want the money go to the minors. Those who want the education go to college. It works for baseball and the money wouldn't make them rich but could lift some families out of poverty. But some would say what about injuries and not making the NFL. The same could be said about those kids who chose to go to college and play for free. Wouldn't all the schools being investigated right now be in different positions right now? I'm pretty sure the college football landscape would be in a lot different place. Just a simple thought.

Paying Attention To Details

Paying attention to details is a trait lost to our youth. Our current generation is spoiled with a sense of entitlement they haven't earned. They have poor work ethics. This includes my own kids for I am as guilty as most parents today of trying to give them more than I had without them earning it. Most kids don't do chores anymore. Some don't even know how to make a bed correctly. What is worse they can't clean a kitchen properly but expect food to be prepared for them or the refrigerator to be full. My grandmother told me it takes less time to do something right the first time, instead of doing stuff over and over again. Do it right the first time and be done with the job or chore. Here is an example I can use about my own kids. I can tell them to wash the dishes. Guess what that is all that will be done. I forget they weren't raise as I was and require more instructions. My grandmother said go wash the dishes and I knew what that meant. It was wash the dishes, take out the trash, wipe down the counters and stove. When that is done sweep and mop the floor. Remember these are the people who you will be relying on to take care of you when you get old or injured. Now look at your children real close. It is a scary thought isn't it? Just a simple thought.

Know It All's

Sometimes being a middle-aged man looking at teenagers wondering did my aunts and uncles look at me the same way. Why does someone 13 to 17 years of age think they have all the answers? It is amazing how someone making no money and paying no bills know everything. These people don't buy their own clothes or food but you can't tell them anything because they know it already. This generation has access to technology we never dreamed was possible. But some of them don't take advantage of these opportunities. Instead they chose to act flip and disrespectful. Let us not forget ungrateful. They take for granted central air and heat or cable television. These kids don't have to go to a library because a laptop has access to all the information they need. But the biggest slap in the face to the older generation is they think it is a right and not a privilege to have a cell-phone. They want everything on it and the most expensive cell-phone with no thought of the bill or plan. Hopefully with age comes wisdom and sense of responsibility. Not only for themselves, but for the sake their children. Just a simple thought.

Wants Vs Needs

When you figure out the difference between what you need and what you want, you should pass that knowledge to your kids. If they learn this lesson at an early age it will save you time and money. Just a simple thought.

Swag

Swag is what this new generation calls their style. Well swag to this forty-something is not a style of dress or slang. Swag is a person who has the ability to be original. The person who is the trendsetter has the swag. This is the person getting paid because all the followers see them and want to be like them. Kids today are by a majority a bunch of followers. Very few have the confidence to be leaders or trendsetters. We as a society are a monkey see monkey do group of people. If you really want swag, learn to think for yourself and not just recite rap lyrics and dress a certain way and think you got swag. Be confident in your abilities. Don't be satisfied to copy someone else. But will this happen anytime soon I think not. The reason is that it takes a little work and maybe a chance of failure. So this generation will just continue their trend of being followers because it is safe. So step up and swag out new generation because I want people who can think out of the box to take us into the future. Just a simple thought.

Wasted Potential

Our kids should be our greatest resource. But we don't use it to our advantage. Why because knowledge is power. With power comes greed, the powerful look for monetary gain instead of enriching this country's future. The nation should get on one page and give all our children the right to the same education so our children's future and their children's future could be brighter. The fact is all kids, not just the rich or well to do kids should be allowed to help raise this country up. Now we have these programs geared to help the children learn at a younger age. For example, the program My Baby Can Read, for the older children there is Sylvan Tutoring. Now when you see something that is advertised, but it never shows the price, guess what? The average family can't afford it. The nation as a whole should get on the same page with teaching our children. The creators of these programs should've by now made their profits. Why not invest in your countries youth? Why can't My Baby Can Read be in every preschool? Public or private, I have seen the ad to this product. Wouldn't it be wonderful if every child could start off with this gift? Think of what these children could accomplish with this knowledge and their imagination. Public school and private schools are on two different playing fields. Private schools get the best of the best, while public schools are just in sad shape. It's not hard to figure that there are more public schools than there are private ones. Think of all the schools in cities like New York, Chicago, Los Angeles, and etc. Even in the smaller cities and communities if all were teaching these programs wouldn't this country be in better shape education wise. Not as long as this type of knowledge is kept by the select few and not the masses. This country is going to be in sad shape. I believe that somewhere in this country there is a group of children who will get this country out of debt and back on track. But not if we miss these bright young minds because we selfishly hold back learning techniques and knowledge that could be taught to all our children. The plan should be simple get one system taught by all the schools, public and private across the nation. Whenever something new arises just add it to the system and tweak it as it progresses. Get the teachers higher salaries. Teachers should be in the league with doctors, lawyers as far as pay. Why, because those are the individuals who will be teaching our future doctors, lawyers, and engineers, police officers, military, and etc. These are just the thoughts of a simple man hoping for a better future for all our children.

New Generation

This new generation must believe life is like a video game. You die and a restart happens and you get another life. It is a shame to see young men, all with unfulfilled potential gone. Why couldn't they just have picked up a book instead of a gun? Imagine what we might have missed already as a human race with the ideas of these young men never realized. Some could have done great things. Now others would or could have changed their way of thinking and sparked the next level in our evolution as a species. But we will never know. Just a simple thought.

CHAPTER 6

Dream

Dreams are what make the everyday struggle of life bearable. If you use each day to make steps towards your dream eventually the journey ends. At that point you realize your dream has become a reality. Just a simple thought.

Co-Pilot

Sometimes you don't need to attach your happiness to another person. Make yourself go each day as a new adventure and sooner or later you will get a co-pilot. The trick is not to look for the co-pilot, but steer the course and the perfect one will come and assist you in your journey. Just a simple thought.

A Person's Heart

The size of a person's heart can't be measured on any metal scale. There are examples of tiny or frail people physically doing amazing things. Sports are where a person's heart is most glorified. But people show their heart in many other ways. People who do those thankless jobs most of us wouldn't think of doing. Those people who risks their lives for strangers, when some wouldn't risk their lives for family. So we can't judge the size of a person's heart after death on a medical scale. But we should judge a person's heart by his or her deeds in life and the character they displayed while they were on this tiny thing called earth. Just a simple thought.

Good Will

Imagine if everyone took the time to do something nice for someone else. I was told once if you can imagine it, you can accomplish it. So imagine everyone helping their fellowman without the promise of reward or payment. It doesn't have to be something big or life changing. Just say something pleasant to a stranger. Smile and nod your head to someone. If you have a buggy full and the person behind you has only one or a couple of items, let them go ahead of you. If more people did some of these little things more often good will and good manners would spread. Maybe some of this good will could knock a dent in some of the greed that is controlling the world we are currently living in. Just a simple thought.

Tested

Being by yourself doesn't mean you are lonely. Knowing what you need to be happy and doing so eliminates loneliness. Being able to educate and entertain yourself is the sign of a strong person. Let's be honest everyone would like a friend to do things with they both enjoy. But there are times in our life when you have to be alone and be strong. Divorce and death of a loved one are the times when your strength will be tested. Even just a bad relationship break-up can test your resolve. But after any of these events you may feel lonely. Take a deep breath and say, I have a ton of things I can be doing. So make a list and hop to it. Once you start going down your list you will be busy and will have no time to feel lonely. As you see things being accomplished, you will notice a change in your feelings. Your heart will feel great and you will begin to glow from an inner joy. Misery loves company, but people are attracted to the opposite. Just a simple thought.

Emergency Brakes

Sometime in life we feel like we are spinning our wheels. Like you are pushing the gas pedal, but not moving. Problem is the emergency brake is up. Find out what your emergency brake is and release it. Once it is released you should be able to move forward with your life. Just a simple thought.

Life Lessons

I have learned a life lesson from my 16 year old son. My son runs on the high school track team. He does different events and one of them is the 300m hurdles. This is his first year doing this event. In his first race he did something I can relate to everyday life. He overcame an obstacle on his way to a second place finish with a smile on his face. While running his race he got to the next to last hurdle, he clipped it and fell. But when he fell he rolled and got right back up. He cleared the next hurdle and finished second. He later told me that he laughed as he fell because he knew it was funny and he still could finish in a top spot. Life will have it's obstacles to overcome. Now when obstacles come my way, I think of my son and think they can only slow me down but not keep me down. Just a simple thought.

Birth Control

There needs to be more daddy's in the world. Birth certificates have a spot for father. Anybody can lay or stand to become a father. Being a daddy is something different. Being a daddy requires work and commitment. Too many documents are blank in the father spot. A lot of the ones with a name are only there so he can have brag about the number of children he has produced. The number of names that are there to be a daddy has to increase. Simple math is that if a daddy is there to give good examples, advice and show the children right from wrong the cycle of crime would decrease. Mothers can do only so much. Children need guidance from both parents or they will find it somewhere else. So before you lie down and make a baby think of what kind of person you want them to be. Think about what kind of love and support you will provide to insure they have a great chance of being a good successful person. If you can't think of what you would do to accomplish this, then maybe you shouldn't lie down to make another person. Just a simple thought.

Hostage

Don't let other people hold your hopes and dreams hostage. They will put obstacles in your way, but as long as you make steps in the right direction, you can overcome those obstacles and reach your destination. Just a simple thought.

CHAPTER 7

Suggestions for the Economic Recovery

Just a few simple suggestions on helping the economy recover.

1.) Instead of the government sending all that money in foreign aid to all those other countries, let's take that money to create jobs here and further assist those suffering from our own natural disasters. Here is one suggestion to see if our elected officials really care about the people who voted them to office.

2.) The governors, congressmen/congress women, and state representatives of each state should work for one dollar a month for two years. Yes, I said it twenty-four dollars for two years. Their salaries could be split between scholarship money for college and the other half put back into the public school's budget of their perspective state. How about cutting back on some of the multiple legislative aid positions and putting that money back in the budget. Be honest do we need our other public servants like policemen, fireman, teachers, correctional officers taking pay cuts.

3.) The average American people faces tough decisions everyday of their lives concerning gas or food. Why should they have to watch the news or read the newspapers and see these oil companies brag about record profits. Since the oil companies have made more than their share of money; the government could regulate a set price, maybe $2.50 a gallon. I am pretty sure that would ease the burden on a lot of us Americans.

But these are the Simple Thoughts of a Simple Man.

Budget Cuts

The President makes a larger salary a year than most of us. The Presidential pension is not a fixed amount, rather it matches the current salary of Cabinet members, which is$191,300 a year as of March 2008. The President used to have secret service detail for life. That ended with Clinton and now just runs for ten years out of office. Now most of us know that most of our public officials were pretty well off in the money before taking office. So why are we paying them these larger than they need pensions, when a person who worked all their life tries to survive off social security and maybe a decent 401 or retirement plan. When these people leave office their salary should stop. We are paying about 5 Presidents right now only the fact that we have only one in office right now is kind of ridiculous. Now the numbers on the other positions has to be greater than 5. Now if the government is spending our taxes on these salaries that are really unnecessary, what else are they wasting it on? Here is a suggestion stop paying millions in salaries to rich people not in office and put it back into healthcare and education. Just a simple thought.

Political Surprises

Is there a reason why politicians always end up with skeletons popping out of the closet at the most unfortunate time? The answer is simple. Whenever someone gets into politics it is not to help your fellow man, but to help yourself. Most of these people have businesses or investments in businesses that would benefit from them holding a certain office. They usually get these positions to pass laws or taxes and regulations to assist themselves or friends and associates or theirs. Now depending on the circumstances they may hold office for a while. They may even keep moving up the political ladder. But once they hit that glass ceiling or decide not to play ball with the majority, amazing things start to happen. All of a sudden that illegitimate child or mistress or even that gay lover jumps out the closet. First denial then the apology ensues. They just realized that they are not untouchable. Everyone in politics have secrets it is just when one of their associates will play that card. All the people within the political network know what the other is doing. Kind of like a check and balance system. Everything stays covered up until they go against the grain. And the funny thing is that their fellow politicians act as if they are shocked and amazed. Now there should be a category at the Oscars for best performance by a politician. Once the cat is out the bag the political career is over. But we are sure none of them will end up broke or on Welfare. Just a simple thought.

Elections

It is getting to the point where we are doing elections just for show. I see where these candidate's campaign has cost this amount of millions all from donations and contributions. I know that is just code for super rich pulling election strings. When is the last time you were asked to donate to a presidential campaign or senator's campaign. Ummm you can't remember and neither can I. Private businesses and or wealthy individuals are funding and backing this elections like owners at the horse races. Why do you think the divide between the haves and the have not's has gotten wider. America used to be the land where every man had a fighting chance to live their dream. Now the rich and powerful have tilted the playing field so much to if you are not born into money you can pretty much forget about living comfortable. They tell you to work hard and do the right thing, but when will they. They have changed laws and regulations to the point they hardly pay taxes or go to jail if they do wrong. They even vote themselves raises and salaries for life. They have the nerve to get on T.V. and act upset and angered about healthcare. If you really want to see them upset, and not just an act. Put the senators and congressmen on medicad and social security and see how soon they could come up with a solution. Cut off those large salaries and pensions and say here $12,000 a year social security and you and your family are covered by medicad. Do you think we would finally get something done or would they just hit up and old college buddy for a bail out like the government did the banks and the car industry. Just a simple thought.

Educated Arrogance

I have been listening to these so called political experts and economist. They make the current president out to be the antichrist. Simple fact is the country was not in great shape when he got in office. I really don't think it is a color thing. It is probably that he is not doing what they want him to do. Let us be real the president is and has been a figure head for the true powers behind the curtain who really are running things. Let's be real a degree in political science and economics are just degrees in double talk and smoke screening. Some of these loud arrogant people with their political radio shows are just jockeying to maybe sneak a peak behind the curtain. Who are you really helping with a degree in either of these fields of study? Not anyone but the person in the mirror. So you can get someone to pay to hear your opinion on either of these topics. You are hoping they pull you in and give you a taste of the pie. You are on television using big words, code for I am just trying to dazzle you. This is done because they know they are not helping the situation or giving a solution. What you are really saying is pay me to bullshit you. You people might as well be magicians or illusionists. The difference is they are trying to entertain us. They have no hidden agenda other than entertaining the crowd. So to all you people with these worthless degrees, how about you get off your butts and contribute to the solution and not just sitting there blowing hot air. Stop wasting our time and resources with the madness and educated arrogance. Do all of us a favor, if you really what to help go get another degree in something useful. If you already have another degree in something useful use it. Just a simple thought.

Millionaire Job Hunting

Why would a millionaire want a job that pays a lot less a year than he makes on his own? Reason is there is an agenda and it is not hidden. Let's just think simple. Get a job to make connections to further your business or businesses. Place friends in places of power to help in the future. Change policies to eliminate the competition. But what happens to the employees of the company? They are known as collateral damage. Just a simple thought.

Burger King or Bust

It was once said if you don't like where you at then leave. Burger King is hiring is what was said. That is an old quote but it means little to those who really think about it. If that was the answer then no one would be unemployed. There would be a Burger King on every corner and everyone who wanted to work would have a job. The problem is not Burger King it is the state of some of our current place of employment. We all know who I am talking about when I say the company. The company used to be a whole body. All the blood, tissue, ligaments and skin have been picked away. Now what remains is only a skeleton. What happens to bones when lack of calcium occurs? They become brittle and break. So to all of us bones left on the skeleton, drink plenty of milk. Maybe we will remain strong enough so we can all land somewhere safe. Those who chose Burger King let's hope they hiring for real. Just a simple thought.

Corporate Takeover

Think for a second on how the corporate takeover works. First upper management sends a scout into the other company to check out the lay of the land then report back. Then upper management arrives at the new company. Now the plan goes into motion. First they bring the rah-rah speeches that they think will reel in the current employees. Then there are sudden changes that turn the workplace into a hostile work environment. Next with the environment changes done, comes the process of pushing out middle management employees out. This is done by making the workplace extremely hostile, so your older employees and the ones with a lot of tenure will get feed up and quit or retire early. Once all of this has taken place, then you will see the employees from the upper management previous company start to filter in. Takeover is now complete. Just a simple thought.

No Retirement

In a matter of 3 years imagine how one person can affect the retirement status and benefits of so many. Imagine walking into a place for 25 years and each day there is a danger of losing your life. You survive all these years and make it to retirement and your reward is gone. The nest egg you envisioned is robbed from you as if you were held up by a common mugger. The compensation for your loyalty and dedications is stripped from you without a second thought. This is the position state employees are in because some multi-millionaire came along and cut their wages, raised their insurance and stole their nest egg. Amazing how someone who could never walk a day in these people's shoes could be so arrogant. How about we go and take the savings and retirement nest egg away from him and his associates? The reason we wouldn't is because they would just go steal it from some other organization. See they would not feel the pain of the people who worked for their retirement, because they would just manipulate the system to keep them in the money. It is sad that people have worked holidays, weekends and shift work to be treated with such disregard. Some of them didn't make it to retirement because they lost their life in the line of duty. WHERE IS THE JUSTICE IN THAT? Just a simple thought.

Technology

Technology is a beautiful thing when used the right way. Some of the things we see in movies and what the government says have just been invented have already been in use. Technology is power. Power creates money. Money becomes involved then greed takes over. So some technology which was invented to help mankind becomes the property of the few until they decide to share it with the world. We simple folks can not imagine what has been invented because we don't wheel the influence or have the so called need to know clearance. Just think about this for a second. How many advances has the cell-phone made in the last 5 years? Now if this is happening at such a quick rate, imagine the other stuff being created they have yet to share with the rest of the world. Just a simple thought.

Why

1. Why do we pay politicians these large salaries and pensions?
2. Why does Congress get to vote themselves raises with our money?
3. Why does the government get to give out contacts to big companies for 2 or 3 times the worth of a product with our money?
4. Why can't we all get the same medical care the politicians are offered?
5. Why has the government gotten away from the original constitution and the concepts of the authors?

Why have we let the select few change the laws and institute new laws to benefit the few and not the many? Just a simple thought.